Family Trees – Unravelling the mystery of your ancestral timeline

Using the map of the past to assist in the living of your future

Rafe Nauen

Copyright © 2014 Rafe Nauen

All rights reserved.

ISBN: 1500573914
ISBN-13: 978-1500573911

DEDICATION

To Isaac Pizer – you started the ball rolling for me, and I am forever grateful, and to Jackie Dunn who simply asked why I hadn't written a book yet!

Contents

Foreword 6

Introduction... 9

Chapter 1 - What is a constellation? 12

Chapter 2 – How did I get into this work, and why does that matter?.. 18

Chapter 3 – The mechanics of a workshop 26

Chapter 4 – Who is the facilitator? 38

Chapter 5 – What is happening to the seeker, before during and after? 39

Chapter 6 – What is going on for the representative, and who might they be?... 41

Chapter 7 – What does a participant need to do? 45

Chapter 8 – Working outside families 48

Chapter 9 – Constellations and chronic health issues........... 50

Chapter 10 – Using stuff other than people to represent in a constellation 55

Chapter 11 – What else do you need to know? 58

ACKNOWLEDGMENTS

It also goes without saying that without the emotional, spiritual, physical and practical support of my wonderful wife Julie Bowman, this book would not exist. And without my family of origin, I wouldn't even exist.

Foreword

I met Paul in 2010. He needed to see me because anger management wasn't hitting the spot. It turned out that he was six weeks old when his grandmother got him adopted to another family. She felt his needs were not being met by his seventeen year old mum. He got a new name and everything. Fifty years on and he was married with children, a father to two stepchildren, and working in the field of his passion – the great outdoors. And yet he was still angry that his mother had not performed the miracle of being what the text books would have a mother be.

I couldn't help him. I never can. It's the individual who needs to help him or herself. What I can do (and did do in his case) was to introduce a set of tools that enabled him to see and feel the rich tapestry of ancestry that had formed him. The particular tool we are talking about in this book is the family constellation workshop developed out of many years' research principally in Germany since the late 1940's.

In Paul's case the dynamics that showed up was the simple relationship between him and his birth mother. So I set them up, with a woman representing Paul's mother, with Paul as himself. Within an hour of the setup, Paul found himself able to truthfully say "Thank you for my life, I got enough"

So what's going on here? How come that was the conclusion? How long does the effect last?

Well three years on Paul is still completely OK, the answer to that question isn't always "forever". In my experience it often is and that means it is an extraordinarily useful tool. The outcome in Paul's case derives from the truth that if you have successfully lived for fifty years, you have children, a long term partner and some stepchildren, then you have been successful with the life you were given, and that had she not had that child, Paul would not have been born. The word "enough" is used often in this work, as it represents the underlying truth – a fire just needs a spark – "just enough" to get it going – what happens later is another matter. With Paul, that spark of life was enough from that particular person for him to a) exist, and b) lead a full and successful life.

"What's going on here?" and "How does it work?" are harder questions to answer, and that really is what this book is about.

Introduction

My name is Rafe Nauen, and I met Isaac Pizer in 2002. My wife Maia had been diagnosed with cancer, and I found myself feeling somewhat responsible – you know, stress causes cancer, I cause stress, and bingo; Maia's cancer must be my fault. Most of my life I had felt responsible – especially for the things that didn't work out, but THIS was a step too far.

I had been researching my family roots, and particularly my German Jewish ancestors, so it seemed entirely appropriate to visit a psychotherapist with a Jewish background. He asked me why I was wanting help, and my answer was that I needed to know what I WAS responsible for and equally what I was NOT responsible for.

Within a few sessions, he could see that a constellation workshop would help. Why? well it became clear that the system I had grown up in (my family of origin) had some difficulties that I needed to clear before I could realistically move on, and just looking at me wasn't going to deal with the underlying issues really. Family counselling was out, as my grandparents were already dead, my parents were distant and unlikely to visit "issues", and the subject of my uncle Richard had come up, but more of that later!

Hence a constellation! I went down to London in November 2002 and began a process that was to yield some extraordinary stories together with some almost unbelievable results, some of which are recounted here, and was to lead me into a whole new career path and involve me in considerable training.

This little book is designed to allay some fears,

and to give a general outline of what you might expect if you were to attend a constellation workshop. It talks of the scope, and who the players in the work might be. If you have found yourself reading to here, you will have come across the concept of the family constellation, and want to know a little more – perhaps just before you attend a workshop. The book has been priced low as a sort of beginner's guide. There are much greater books on the subject that deal with metaphysics, and with the orders of love, but here I have kept that to a bare minimum. Enjoy the stories in this book, and please attend workshops – even if you aren't a seeker, they reveal extraordinary elements of life itself, which especially the western civilisation has for the most part, skimmed over.

Chapter 1 - What is a constellation?

Why is that important in a book about constellations? Well it reveals the journey that leads us to do this work in the first place, and in my case, and in so many others, it reveals an example of the different road taken after undertaking this work.

So, what is a constellation (apart from a group of stars) – well fundamentally, it's a living map that reveals the hidden dynamics of any system. A system is any group defined by the relationship they have to each other – family, workgroup, board of directors and so on. In this book, I am concentrating on family systems, but the rules even apply to any grouping of people or things that might be regarded as a system – even down to a chronic illness – that will be discussed in a later chapter, but by way of example someone has a painful broken leg. Clearly the problem is in the leg, or perhaps they are even more precise and say their knee is the issue, but their lack of mobility will have a profound effect on what they are able to do. They might have suffered some severe trauma getting the damaged knee, so could have nightmares, quite apart from the normal sleep deprivation from pain. That may mean that they get annoyed or upset more than would be normal for them. The family then will have to rally around – transport, maybe the bedroom is inaccessible so things will change in the house, and maybe there is a sudden drop in income that coincides with a sudden increase in costs, so worry in the family will increase. So you can see that looking at basic elements on their own is a far from perfect way to arrive at successful outcomes, and sometimes it can be far more useful to look at the system.

The starting point is always someone who wants to look at an issue, perhaps there's a recurrent problem at work, or some situation that they can't quite come to grips with. It may be a forced change within the system – a death, a birth, a marriage or a divorce, or "problems" with a child's behaviour may becoming noticeably difficult to deal with. Constellations are a powerful way of working with such issues. Rather than look at the individual or the place where the problem is, we look at the whole system. That's because an individual is always part of a much wider interconnected system, and the problem may just be a symptom of something that's actually happening elsewhere. That was exactly true in my case, and I shall be using my own experience as well as other people's whose constellations I have facilitated further on in this book.

What we do is set up a visual spatial representation of that system. Ideally we use people to represent the different parts of the system so it becomes a living map or constellation, but pieces of felt on a floor, post it notes or even PlayPeople™ can be used. We then ask those representatives to listen to their feelings, their sensations and their intuitions and what happens is that the underlying dynamics of the system come to the surface. It seems that simply the client giving permission for an element of their existence to be represented is enough for the display of the dynamics to begin. Many hundreds of thousands of workshops have been noted and written up, and they all show that some hidden dynamics have been revealed that have lain hidden previously.

Constellations relies on some underlying principles - a bit like a house relies on gravity.

1. Everyone has an equal right to belong - everyone who enters a system (a new baby for example) has a right to as much love as anyone else, and it can be shown that having "favourites" causes issues down the line

2. Things that come before have to give way to things that come later - an older sibling has to allow his or her world to change a little for the survival of the system, and his or her place within it.

3. Later systems take precedence over older systems. If someone has a child in the context of an affair, it can be pretty harsh for the original family system. The person who has partially moved away and into a new system, will have much more energy for the new system, whatever they say to themselves, or whatever promises they may make.

4. The balance of giving and receiving needs to be maintained - common sense (and a great deal of research) has shown that balance must be maintained in all things, especially family systems.

In the high profile case of Maddie McCann, many people have commented that the extent of what the parents will do/ have done for Maddie attempts to balance what was not done prior to her sudden absence. What they have done for Maddie, cannot be replicated with the other two children without loss, and that is an example of the hidden laws of love, which pervade this work.

Chapter 2 – How did I get into this work, and why does that matter?

This chapter is to explain how someone might find themselves as a constellation practitioner. I am not a qualified psychotherapist, and for the training, that is not necessary.

I was born into a middle class family where hard work and ambition were important. My mother miscarried her first child, then had Richard and then three and a half years later she had me. Nine years after that my sister was born. My father had ambition for his children, and being a self-aware little boy, I found myself often at odds with that ambition – if I did well, he would expect me to do even better, so rewards were extremely rare – it felt like I would never succeed in impressing him. At first I attempted to get that approval, but gradually, as I realised it would always be out of reach I began to play up. I thought it was just them, and how life was, until my sister was born. When she arrived, I realised that it was me! She was showered with the apparent love I craved.

I found that sabotage was the most powerful weapon in my armoury – I couldn't necessarily win, but I certainly could fail in someone else's terms. And I could do that all by myself!

I began a succession of career paths that just fulfilled my enjoyment of life, and my naturally inquisitive nature. I was a farmer, a lorry driver, a coach driver, I went to university late on, and passed my degree (my parents didn't attend the graduation because the university was then "only a polytechnic!") I became a business consultant, the financial director of a hotel, the chairman of a housing association, an IT consultant, and so on. Work on myself – psychological and spiritual – had been part of my personal ambition since leaving home at 17 – driven by disappointment in the "way my parents had done it"

I was married at 20, and had two children. 10 years later we had divorced due to my wife having had several affairs. Naturally I found myself also feeling responsible, and "not being good enough" had been a familiar theme throughout my childhood. The divorce was messy, but I dusted myself off and got on with the next phase – which included being chairman of the Bristol Liberal party. I was still at university, and remarried – this time to Maia. We had three children, and Maia also miscarried one child. Interestingly, my mother's miscarriage seems to have been important to the system, in that my brother was really the second child, not the first. Naturally when a first child dies along the way to being born, the parents are devastated, whereas in Maia's case, we had decided not to have more children, and then the ensuing pregnancy and subsequent miscarriage led us to conclude that a third child was indeed welcome, so in that case, the miscarriage paved the way for our youngest child to be welcomed into our family, instead of perhaps being resented as a "mistake".

In 2002 Maia, who had had experience of abuse in her early life, became ill, and the diagnosis was cancer. Our relationship had been difficult, despite both being on the same page about our children, our spirituality, and support for each other's careers. We just seemed to argue a lot. I felt blamed for many things, just as in my early childhood, so when Maia got the diagnosis, I felt responsible. I needed help, and found Isaac. We worked through what I was, and perhaps more importantly, what I was not responsible for, and soon realised that my issues belonged to a wider system than just me.

As in all things, aspects can be observed from the minutiae in the microcosm, right up to the macrocosm. Take cancer for example. Someone with a breast cancer diagnosis can correctly talk of the cancer affecting:

- The cells in the tumour
- The tumour
- Her breast
- Her body
- Her life
- Her relationship
- Her family
- The communities she belongs to

In my case, Isaac saw the issues I presented as systemic, and indicating stuff that went back to earlier life, and perhaps even before I was born, and so quickly recommended that I attend a constellation workshop.

I attended a constellation with Richard Wallstein, and after the initial conversation, found myself setting up my mother, father, brother and my mother's brother Richard who had died three days before his twenty first birthday. The Fairey Fulmar plane he was flying failed and he crashed, killing himself and the navigator. The family, amidst that tragedy, put him on an unassailable pedestal. He would never grow old they said. Naturally when my mother became pregnant she named the new baby Richard in honour of a handsome man, who had changed the whole balance of the whole family by dying young, and in some way to put back something into the gaping hole that the death of the young pilot had caused. During the constellation, it became clear that there was an unhealthy balance with my mother and her brother, but that was all the information we had. The important parts of the constellation for me were the shifts in balance – the fact that as a middle aged man, with five children, all healthy and doing their own thing in their own lives, I could regard myself as successful – that I had got enough, and perpetually enquiring in my mind as to what I had and had not got from my parents had become fruitless – I had had exactly enough to become the person I was at that moment.

In 2004 Maia died, and Richard surprisingly attended the funeral. He had been distant for some time, so I hadn't expected him to make the difficult journey in early January. In September that year he committed suicide. He was living a good life in Fuertaventura but suspected he had a prostate issue, and rather than face being imperfect, or ill, killed himself. I was to discover some years later that my uncle Richard did not die in a tragic accident due to a technical fault, but rather that my uncle had been experimenting with unauthorised low flying over the airfield, and killed himself and his navigator by crashing into another Fairey Fulmar plane. Richard had died young, being stupid, but got revered as a tragic hero within the family – in the squadron where two out of six planes were bust by his antics, I suspect he was regarded as an idiot. My brother was brought up in the image of unassailable perfection that would never grow old – ironic! And whilst that fact cannot be seen as a blame tool, it certainly provides a backdrop for living out certain realities. Clearly many things *could* have happened that might have changed that fate. He could have discovered the truth about his uncle namesake and changed his name – names are important, and sometimes *that* important! It would be a brave person to name their new born son Adolf even seventy years on from the Second World War. Knowing those simple truths, and honouring them (finding a place for them) could have meant there were different choices apparently available. The choices that Richard made, based on the knowledge he had, led him to an early death, whatever the justifications to himself.

Chapter 3 – The mechanics of a workshop

What happens in a constellation workshop? I am going to use a real example from a workshop held some years ago

Who is in a constellation?

1. The facilitator – someone who guides the process, but who remains as far as possible, outside the process
2. A seeker - someone who feels the urge to look at their stuff, right now – they will probably be a bit fired up, enthusiastic – their moment has arrived.
3. Representatives – people who will get asked to represent other people during the process – placeholders certainly, but sometimes quite a bit more
4. Participants – the rest of the people in the workshop – they sit around the edge of the working area and hold the energy – they just observe mostly – they will get a chance to be a seeker, or a participant later

Only the facilitator will necessarily have had prior experience of constellation work, but some, maybe all of the others will have attended workshops before – even participants get a big learning from the work.

Everyone sits around in a circle of chairs – preferably about 18-20 feet across the circle. The facilitator will have picked a place to sit, and have a vacant chair next to him or her. He or she will probably do a short meditation, so that everyone is calm, relaxed and body conscious – by that I mean that people become aware of what is going on in their own body, so that they can express changes that occur – these may become quite important as the work progresses. The circle inside the chairs is called the field – like a field of energy, and is identified to establish boundaries to the work.

Firstly, a seeker is chosen. The facilitator may

choose, or ask who is ready, or maybe another method is used. The seeker comes and sits by the facilitator. For this example, let's say the seeker is female and forty-six years old, and the facilitator is me! This movement symbolises moving into a place where other things become enabled. The seeker then tells the facilitator the facts. The facilitator is not interested in blame, or opinion, just facts – such as my mother and father are still alive; they separated when I was two, and I haven't seen my father since that day; my mother had two miscarriages before I was born, but I have an older brother that survived. My mother remarried when I was two and a half.

What the facilitator is doing here is to identify the important elements in what was around during the seekers early life – more importance is placed on things that happened in the family before the seeker was born, because those things will have moulded the seeker. The facilitator will no doubt make a judgement call on whether to set up the mother's new husband at the outset, or to see if he figures later. Again, a judgement call will be required to reckon whether the miscarriages are significant – sometimes they are and sometimes they aren't. In this work, we find that abortions always have a place, still births always have a place, and miscarriages do only sometimes.

So I ask the seeker what is her burning desire (or some such form of words) – this enables an intention to be set, and is useful but not essential to the work. She says "All my relationships die too soon". She says she has a mother (still alive) a father (still alive) and an elder brother. She thinks her mother had a miscarriage between her brother and her. I ask her to choose four people to represent herself, her mother, her father, and her brother. I choose not to complicate matters just yet by requesting a representative of the miscarried baby. It is simpler for me to work if the representatives are women for women and men for men, but in truth it is not important. I have run several constellations where there were a lot of one sex, and insufficient of the other for that rule to apply. A basic fundamental of the work is "Working with what is" – in other words we all have to survive and succeed with whatever deal of cards we get – we can make the best of it, just as easily as the worst of it. I know a woman whose father was a real bully. He terrorised her but she learned to stick out her jaw, and say "Yeah, that all you got?" many years later she was on the front line at Greenham Common when an American soldier pointed a machine gun at her. She was part of thousands of women campaigning to not have American missiles launched from English soil without our involvement in a war. She stuck out her jaw and suggested "Go on then, pull the trigger if you've got the balls" Of course he backed down. She had learned to resource herself from her terrible experiences as a child.

So what happens next? I ask her to set the representatives up – by which I mean she asks them if they are willing to act as a representative. If they say yes, they stand up and she stands behind them with hands lightly on their shoulders, and she moves them to a place in the field (the space within the circle of chairs) that "feels right". Extraordinarily, whilst it sounds odd, there is such a place, and so far, no-one in a workshop has ever struggled to find such a place!

So now we have four people standing up, in the circle, and the seeker now sits down to watch, to listen and to feel. She cannot interrupt, or even interject – but I may ask confirmation of things that I see, or for more information when something odd crops up.

The seeker's rep is standing alone in the middle, the father is standing near the edge looking out, the mother is near the edge looking in, towards the father and the brother is near the middle, again looking towards the father. So what can I work on? Let's make some assumptions. One of the beauties of this work is that we can test hypotheses readily and easily without any ecological damage (i.e. we can experiment without any problems occurring further down the line). I suggest that dad would rather be somewhere else (in constellation speak, he wishes to leave) Dad relaxes immediately and even moves to do just that, leave. I ask him where his interest lies – he says comrades. I ask the seeker if she has any idea what this means, because it means nothing to me, nor to the participants and representatives present at this workshop, not even the representative that uttered the word!

She says "my dad worked on a minesweeper in the war, and he was called away for some important work on another ship, and whilst he was gone his ship went down with all hands on deck. He was devastated and felt he should have died with his comrades"

I ask three people to stand just outside the circle near the dad, to represent the comrades who died. They seem happy, and not troubled, which surprises all of us, especially dad! I ask him to talk to them, and for them to respond. A dialogue ensues where it becomes clear that dad surviving felt good to the others – he got a life, a beautiful daughter and for him to have died would have stopped that and that would have been in no-one's interest.

So what's going on here? People who have never met, are having a conversation that they could never have had and would never happen in reality. It displays a general attitude to death, and has a distinct relationship with understanding and relieving survivor guilt. And that element of the situation wasn't even known at the outset, so how did dad's representative come up with "Comrades"?

It seems that we carry with us a metaphysical energy that contains truths and aspects that protect us and keep us safe in our journey. Sometimes the trauma surrounding such things becomes outmoded and can safely be dropped. When we "set people up" in a constellation we are handing over permission for a small part of that energy to be replicated within a virtual map, and gives us the ability to observe, and to change those energies.

Humans are unusual in that nearly everything they take into later life is borne out of a loyalty to parenting – maybe not actual father and mother, but the process of parenting which means that children learn to become adults, and eventually become adults with whatever they have picked up along the way.

I have noticed that dad's representative is

wanting to turn towards the field – I suggest he follows that movement, and I can see that he is looking warmer. I suggest some words he might say. This is a facilitator technique for uncovering some historical truths. We can suggest words, and then when they have said, ask the person who said them to say if they felt true. Surprisingly, they will probably have a strong feeling either way – very seldom an "I'm not sure" In this case I ask him to say to his daughter "I didn't know you were there" the seekers rep bursts into tears. He offers a hug, and they hold an embrace for a while. The other reps have turned to look, and the brother's rep is crying a little too. Mum look radiant.

In this short exercise, it has become clear that the most important perceived relationship for the father was to his dead comrades, and thus it becomes clear that the daughter – our seeker here, has spent her life so far looking for relationships that become dead out of love for her dad, and that to have been associated with life and vibrancy would have been disloyal. Clearly this is errant nonsense. However, what has happened here is that everything has changed in a short space of time. The representatives are thanked and they sit down. I suggest that chatter is minimal, and that discussion about who did what to who and why should be let go of. The work has begun, but has not yet ended. The seeker now has to allow the change to permeate her body and mind, such that every cell has a very slightly different outlook. That can take time, and is best done with space, and not clamour. I also suggest that for confidentiality reasons that any discussion of the works should definitely include this piece of work, but with enough detail removed or changed to protect identities completely – just as I have in this book.

So feedback from this particular piece of work – the seeker can have a relationship with someone who wishes very much to be alive, and for the relationship itself to be alive. The mother has seen what she intrinsically knew was there already, and the son has been seen, and can now model himself on a father that wishes to be present. And the father can breathe again! Instead of feeling every day that he should have died with his comrades – the message to his daughter gets to feel like it would have been more correct if she had not been born – hardly a healthy paradigm to live under!

There is an underlying truth with the loyalty thing. If you are a man, you should ideally be a bit like your dad and marry someone a bit like your mum. Equally, if you are a woman you should be a bit like your mum, and marry someone a bit like your dad. In many cases that is observable fact, and I have even observed a gay man whose partner was quite a bit like his mum in attitudes and personality even. If you look around, it is common enough for this to be true!

Chapter 4 – Who is the facilitator?

Like me, a facilitator is likely to have done a fair bit of work psychotherapeutically on themselves over some time and have come to constellations out of personal need, and then developed into a facilitator from some training. Training in the UK is not widely available, there are no specific qualifications as such, and because the work avoids the facilitator becoming an expert in someone's life as a psychotherapist might. Many constellations are carried out with people who have never met the facilitator or the participants before, and may never again. They may need no aftercare, and it will have been the other people than the facilitator that have done all the representational work for the client (seeker). They will need to be quite good managers of people and time, because although some participants may not get to work during a day's workshop, everyone needs to go home feeling satisfied.

Chapter 5 – What is happening to the seeker, before during and after?

The seeker arrived at the workshop full of hopes and fears – would he get to do any work? Would he be able to express what it is he needed to look at? Would the courage he had built up dissipate at the crucial moment? Would he be any good as a representative? Would the work actually change anything? – He had lived with the apparent issues for over 40 years, how on earth could a day in a room with 10 total strangers change at all?

All the doubts, concerns and apprehensions I have mentioned in this book, are very real, and absolutely normal in this work. There is an innate belief that an hour's work is very unlikely to change the effects of a lifetime, and perhaps generations of lead up to this moment. Perhaps now would be a moment to re-read the foreword of this book. Paul's story is very real, (name changed but little else). And how does he feel now? That his life has changed immensely for the better.

In the same way that a representative feel very much the reality of the things that he or she feels, hears and sees during the work, the seeker feels utterly involved. He or she will often express the emotional build up with tears of sadness, laughter or release. The words expressed by the representatives and the feelings expressed by them feel just as real as if they had been expressed by the very people they are representing. Thus the seeker will go through an extraordinary journey during the process. They fast track a relearning of the truths behind the world that they come from and in so doing allow themselves to shift gear in life, and to evolve. Sometimes the process is spectacularly fast.

Chapter 6 – What is going on for the representative, and who might they be?

The participants have come to a workshop in the hope of resolving a long standing issue that they have come to realise is bigger than just them – it belongs to a system they are a member of. They have never attended a group therapy session before, and they are apprehensive. They have been told that a) it will help, and b) they may never feel quite the same again! On one hand, great! On the other, pretty scary. For this example, the facilitator is female, and the participant male.

The facilitator has spoken for 10 minutes about the work, what to expect, what to not expect, its origins and some examples from workshops she has facilitated. (Greater and scarier already) and then he finds himself being asked to represent a grandfather who died mysteriously 20 years before the seeker was born, but on some whim of the facilitator, appears to be relevant to the seeker's story. Scepticism rules at this moment.

The seeker stands behind him and physically but gently adjusts the direction and flow of movement to an apparent "right place" – comfort zones are being adjusted by now!

And then he feels it. Something wrong about the place, noticing something that would make him "feel" better, and decidedly odd. At last the facilitator asks, and how is X? At last an opportunity to say what has become burning inside. "I feel all wrong here" "so move to where you feel better" he does, but during the process steps back into the person who came here for his own work, and notices how odd this process is. He has now found a place that feels "right" – decidedly odd that that should ever be true within a circle of chairs, and yet it is true.

Then the facilitator is asking others how that feels now that grandpa is over there. Again, decidedly odd. And they have answers! Gradually the process reveals itself, and the juxtapositions change and evolve to a setup that looks and feels perfectly OK to all the representatives standing up, and to all the participants still sitting on chairs. The mood has changed, the seeker is laughing and crying and something has shifted. An unseen, hidden element has moved into clear sight, or left completely and everyone feels elated. Extraordinary! The constellation has ended and less than an hour has flown by – judging by the people who represented, an eon has gone by. There is some discussion, a reminder of confidentiality and for the participant, all anxiety and concern has vanished. For the seeker, they just feel different, inexplicably.

The facilitator explains. She says that what happened here is that the seeker gave permission to some generous people for them to represent the different people that have moulded the seeker's life. With that generosity came an innate knowledge of some stuff that will matter for the seeker. She suggests that we just accept, and don't question what comes up. Let her be the arbiter of that. That freedom enables truths to come out. Truth in this work tends to be checked in that something that is true, when we hear it, tends to make us feel better, stronger, warmer etc., and conversely things that are not true tend to make us feel cooler, weaker etc. In this work those checks are good enough, because as each representative only has internal representations to go on, they are very useful pieces of the jig saw puzzle of their lives.

Chapter 7 – What does a participant need to do?

Everyone except the facilitator is a participant in this work. The facilitator will have been trained over some years, the others may never have been even close to this work before. A participant can become a seeker when then facilitator asks who would like to work, and a participant can become a representative when the seeker asks people to represent people in his or her constellation. The rest remain participants for the duration of that particular piece of work, which typically lasts about an hour. They sit on the chairs around the circle, and they provide a boundary to the work. Clearly 6 people sitting randomly around a circle of chairs has more definition than just the chairs, or an open space, so it can be seen that this is an important element to the work. Sometimes in a workshop, a participant will say to me "Excuse me, but I think

I may be involved in this constellation" For me that is very helpful, because it will likely unblock an area that hitherto hadn't been seen. What has happened to that person? They just felt connected – just like you meet someone sometime and feel sure you have met them before, but even after excessive calendar hunting, you conclude that this is indeed the first meeting. It sometimes gets explained as "we must have met in a past life"! It's just a recognition of connection. And that is very useful here, as hidden elements always have agendas of their own. Take family secrets. Often in this work a secret comes up – "Uncle Albert – well they never talked about him, something about the war, but I never was sure what it was". Sometimes it is enough just to identify the secret as a secret that belongs to another time, another place, or another person, and simply let it go, without ever knowing what the secret was. But sometimes, when someone is refused the right to belong to a system – in this case Albert, something that comes later in the system will honour him out of a need for everything to be balanced (just like the oceans are balanced overall, and if there are highs in Hawaii then there will be lows in Devon). The participant who revealed a connection (and has therefore just become a representative) has brought in that balance, and enabled it to be honoured.

The truth is that things that came before – all of it is part of the landscape that made us exactly who we are, and if we reject any of the past, we reject ourselves.

Chapter 8 – Working outside families

It is common for an issue at work, or in a group of any sort, to be in the realm of the whole group, and not just an individual within that group. The value of the constellation is that managers can experiment with ideas and tease out elements that increase poor consequences, and enhance good ones. I have worked with sales managers who saw immediately that they had become embroiled in office stuff, and that they needed to face outwards from the centre so that they could draw in business from the outside world, rather than scurry around in the mechanics of the organisation to which they belonged, creating issues and moaning rather a lot. The work evolves in exactly the same way, (unless using stuff other than people to represent – see chapter 10) with one manager setting up him or herself and setting others up to represent the other elements identified during the initial conversation between the seeker and the facilitator. Ideally, such constellations are set up with a number of managers or owners from different firms coming together to explore their own businesses. The main difference between a family constellation and a business one is that very often in the business one, other elements come in. Suppliers, money, government regulation, quality etc. It can be seen in a constellation with John Lewis, quality would be important and with their slogan of never knowingly undersold, value for money is crucial, but the same constellation with Poundland would have no place for quality, and the value simply has to be to sell profitably for under a pound. So whilst both are retail stores and both have the same underlying motive – to be a profitable business for shareholders – the elements within the business are significantly different. A similar style book on the subject of business constellations is being prepared.

Chapter 9 – Constellations and chronic health issues

As in the case of someone with a broken leg, we can see the issue in terms of the leg itself, the body, the family or the community including hospital, ambulances, doctors etc.

But let's take a genuine example from experience.

A woman came to me for help. She was in her thirties, and had had a diagnosis of breast cancer. She had not had children, and wanted to treat the cancer with alternative therapies, hence her coming to me.

She came to me as a client for general counselling. From the outset it could be seen that any resolution involved deeper issues than had been identified so far, so I suggested a constellation to map the elements. She set up herself, her mother, her father and her health.

What immediately became apparent was that her health was not properly attached to her, and seemed to be a floating element that belonged somewhere back in her family, back in India even. As with all constellation representatives, they can be asked questions, and sometimes those answers are revealing. In her case, the health had been given to its rightful owner – back before she was born there were issues surrounding health in the family, and it gave rise to a need for someone to "take it on"

She is not out of the woods yet, but the journey has become massively simpler and easier, and she is most certainly on a road to recovery!

Whilst one example is not conclusive proof, it shows the direction of travel! Picture a scenario. A woman has spent quite a large proportion of her adult life thinking about and caring for her children. They grow up, and leave home, and she suffers from "empty nest syndrome" and that coincides with menopausal symptoms. She begins to feel a bit useless, would need to retrain if she were to go back to the commerce she left some years before. She has for the children's benefit worked as a teaching assistant in the intervening years. Then she begins to regain her relationship with her mother – they start doing things together and she starts doing more for her mother fulfilling that caring role she misses. She makes comments such as, "don't worry, I'll see to it . . ." then her mother gets ill and she begins to help her get to doctors, to hospitals and starts doing her shopping. "Don't worry mum I'll do it for you". That begins a downward slide towards the "I'd rather die than let anything happen to my mum!"

With that statement comes a risk. We are all prone to the diseases and symptoms of the human experience, and inviting it in is a potentially crazy thing to do – words expressed are important, and we need to understand the effects – a personal beef is with Race for Life with the slogan "Cancer – we are coming to get you" Why would anyone in their right mind go and get cancer?"

So back to the scenario – and remember loyalty and now we have "I'll do it for you" our lady begins herself to feel unwell – she has a chronic illness that does not belong to her, and the constellation work will a) reveal its identity, but b) also enable a reestablishment of correct responsibility. It never helps someone else to take on their illness, it merely duplicates it.

So a dialogue can be found between the donor, the illness and the recipient, and an evolution can take place. Stephan Hausner has done extensive research in Germany around this issue – and it is worth reading his book "Even if it costs me my life"

The dialogue and change of juxtaposition between the players in this scenario enables change. Change of mind-set, change of dynamics within the system, and indeed the body, and therefore, a healing, which in these circumstances is about as good as it gets.

Chapter 10 – Using stuff other than people to represent in a constellation

Using people to represent other people and elements within a system enables a flow of dialogue and energy together with emotions. But that doesn't mean that other things can't be used as representatives.

In certain circumstances the work needs to be done in a one to one environment, and therefore representing the elements with people is out of the question. In these cases, we can use an array of things.

Felts – pieces of felt that identify gender by shape and direction by a small cut-out are commonly used by practitioners. The felts are placed on the floor by the seeker, and he/she adjusts them and stands on them to sense the message to be learned from each element. I have worked with felts with family constellation and business constellations alike – both to extraordinarily good purpose.

Blocks – small square and around chunks of plastic that can be used on a table top – again many constellation facilitators use these to generate a virtual map of the system, and then to use the process of modifying the map by simply shifting pieces around to change the underlying dynamics of the system. People who have witnessed this work find it quite extraordinary in its effects.

Figures – playpeople are sold in Family Constellation sets, so common is their usage in constellation work. They break down the barriers of resistance to new ideas by their very simplicity. They can also be used to great effect with Children – I have worked with a four-year-old, whose parents had recently split up and whose daddy now had a new partner. The work showed what his position in the whole system was, and it enabled him to see that a) it had never been his fault, and b) that he still had a very important place in set of interrelated systems. He was too unsophisticated to understand a) but 3 years on he still has never felt like that, and working with children of divorced parents in the past, I have seen it as very common thread.

Chapter 11 – What else do you need to know?

How do you get to know about constellations workshops? – Google "constellations" and your towns name, visit www.rafenauen.com email me at rafe@rafenauen.com or call me on 01332 232756 for a chat about what the next step is.

You could also have a Skype constellation – go to skype-constellations.com

The only book I have referred to in this book is Stephan Hausner – "Even if it costs me my life" ISBN 978-0415898058

There are many books on constellations from all over the world. Check out www.hellinger.com – Bert Hellinger has done much pioneering work in Germany over the last 50 years.

ABOUT THE AUTHOR

Rafe Nauen was born in 1950 in Orpington Kent. He is married to Julie Bowman and has 7 children and 9 grandchildren. He works in Derby as a constellation facilitator to private and business customers, and runs retreats in Kefalonia Greece, where people can find out quite a bit more about who they really are.

Printed in Great Britain
by Amazon